P9-CLC-441

the great *sushi* and sashimi cookbook

Published in Canada 2001 by Whitecap Books

For more information, contact Whitecap Books

351 Lynn Avenue, North Vancouver, BC V7J 2C4

Project Manager: Anthony Carroll

Food Photography: Warren Webb

Sushi Chefs: Masakazu Hori and Kazu Takahashi

Food Stylists: Kazu Takahashi and Masakazu Hori

Recipe Development: Kazu Takahashi and Masakazu Hori

Creative Director: Paul Sims

Design: Paul Sims

Proofreader: Andrea Tarttelin

All rights reserved. No part of this book may be stored, reproduced or transmitted in any form or by any means
without written permission of the publishers, except in the case of brief quotations embodied in critical articles and reviews.
The publishers would like to thank Mr. Kazu Takahashi and his staff of the Sushi Bar Rashai, authentic Japanese Restaurant at
241 Parramatta Road, Annandale NSW, for his help and assistance in the compilation of this book.

National Library of Canada Cataloguing in Publication Data

Hori, Masakazu, 1970-

The Great Sushi and Sashimi Cookbook

Includes Index

ISBN 1 55285 234 2

1. Sushi. 2. Cookery, Japanese. 3. Cookery (Seafood)

I. Takasashi, Kazu, 1954- II. Title.

TX724.5.J3H67 2001   641.5952   C2001-910887-7

This edition printed July 2001

Computer typeset in: Humanist, Skia and Garamond Italic

Printed in China

contents

introduction

Sushi

It's a mystery. How can something so simple seem so incredibly complicated?

If you're a new to sushi, it's no wonder you're a little intimidated. There's the language, the customs . . . and what a dazzling array of ways to put rice and fish together! Rice cubes topped with all manner of sea delicacies . . . bite-size kelp rolls . . . little seaweed "boats."

Your friends, of course, are no help at all. Half swear they hate the stuff, particularly those who haven't tried it, and the ones who love it are too enthused over the anago (sea eel) or raving about uni (sea urchin - see glossary on page 120) to help a novice make a less exotic selection.

But the biggest hurdle - when you come "face to fin" with your first sushi experience - is knowing what you're getting into. Not to worry. All you need is a few more facts and a little less attitude. Just a couple of tips about how to navigate these new waters. By reading this book you will not only learn how to make sushi, but you will get some insight to the whole sushi experience.

Sushi Origin

Japan is an island nation, its surrounding seas warmed by Kuroshio, the plankton-rich Japan Current, and abundant with an astonishing variety of fish and shellfish. The islands themselves are mountainous, and what little arable land exists is terraced and carefully cultivated to coax rice and a few other crops. Japan has always fed its dense population from the sea and the rice fields, its cuisine emphasising what nature provides. Sushi, the combination of raw fish and seasoned rice that seems so exotic to foreigners, is a supremely logical food in Japan.

Sushi began centuries ago in Japan as a method of preserving fish. It is told that the origins of sushi came from countries of Southeastern Asia. Cleaned, raw fish were pressed between layers of salt and weighted with a stone. After a few weeks, the stone was removed and replaced with a light cover, and a few months after that, the fermented fish and rice were considered ready to eat. Some restaurants in Tokyo still serve this original style of sushi made with freshwater carp called narezushi.

Its flavour is so strong that it obscures the identity of the fish altogether, and narezushi is something of an acquired taste.

It wasn't until the eighteenth century that a clever chef named Yohei decided to forgo the fermentation and serve sushi in something resembling its present form. It became very popular and two distinct styles emerged Kansai style, from the city of Osaka in the Kansai region, and Edo style, from Tokyo, which was then called Edo. Osaka has always been the commercial capital of Japan, and the rice merchants there developed sushi that consisted primarily of seasoned rice mixed with other ingredients and formed into decorative, edible packages. Tokyo, located on a bay then rich with fish and shellfish, produced nigiri-zushi, featuring a select bit of seafood on a small pad of seasoned rice. Although the ornamental sushi of the Kansai region is still very popular, it is nigiri-sushi that foreigners are most familiar with.

basic essentials

Equipment

This is a basic set of utensils for making sushi.

Rice-cooling tub (Hangiri)

Is used for cooling the vinegared rice giving it the perfect texture and gloss. It is made of cypress bound with copper hoops, but any wooden or plastic vessel can be used instead.

Spatula (Shamoji)

Is used to turn and spread sushi rice while cooling it. Traditionally the spatula is a symbol of the housewife's position in the household. You can use an ordinary spoon instead, wooden or plastic.

Fan (Uchiwa)

Is used to drive off moisture and encourage evaporation to get the right texture and flavour of sushi rice. Originally this fan is made of bamboo ribs covered with either paper or silk. If no fan is available, a piece of cardboard or a magazine can be used instead.

Bowl

A large bowl with a lid is necessary to store the cooked sushi rice in order to keep it warm while making your sushi.

Chopping board (Manaita)

This is a must. Traditionally made of wood, but nowadays many people prefer chopping boards made of rubber or resin. These are easier to keep clean.

Chopsticks (saibashi)

Basically there are two types of chopsticks. Long chopsticks for cooking, often made from metal, are useful once they are mastered, for picking things up and shorter chopsticks for eating.

Tweezers

Used to remove small bones from fish. Larger, straight-ended tweezers are better than smaller variety commonly found in the bathroom and can be obtained from fish markets or specialty stores.

Rolling mat (Makisu)

Made of bamboo woven together with cotton string, this is used to make rolled sushi.

Knives

The only way to get nicely cut surfaces is to use steel knives of good quality. Use whetstones, and sharpen the blades yourself. Good Japanese knives are an outgrowth of forging the Japanese sword which is world famous for its sharpness. The knives are a chef's most valuable possessions and sushi chefs keep a wet cloth near by, frequently wiping the blades to keep their knives clean as they work. Here are the basic types:

Cleavers (Deba-bocho)

Are wide heavy knives with a triangular-shaped blades capable of cutting bone.

Vegetable knives (Nakiri-bocho)

Are lighter than cleavers and the blade is rectangular in shape.

Fish knives (Sashimi-bocho)

Are long and slender. The pointed type is most popular in Osaka and the blunt-ended type is most popular in Tokyo. Excellent for filleting and slicing fish, they are also just right for slicing rolled sushi.

ingredients

Sugared water or any alcoholic beverage, allowed to stand long enough, naturally sours and becomes vinegar. The word in itself is French and comes from vin (wine) and aigre (sour). In Japan it is made from rice, the grain from which sake is brewed. With the power to alter proteins, vinegar destroys bacteria. Adding sugar to sushi rice is to prevent the tartness of vinegar from coming through too strongly.

Soy Sauce

Soy sauce is popular all over the world, used under many appellations: all flavour, meat sauce, all purpose seasoning etc. Japanese soy sauce, rather than the darker and richer Chinese variety, is the one for sushi lovers. Soy sauce is highly recommended as a natural fermented food, superior to salt, sugar or synthetic seasonings. It is essential to most traditional Japanese foods, including sushi, tempura, sukiyaki and noodles.

To tell good soy sauce from bad, use the following guidelines:

Aroma. A good soy sauce never produces an unpleasant smell, no matter how deeply you inhale.

Colour. When a small quantity is poured into a white dish, good soy sauce looks reddish.

Clarity. Good soy sauce is perfectly translucent. Sunlight passing through it gives it a lovely glow.

Once opened, soy sauce should be stored in a cool, dark, dry place or refrigerated.

Pickled Ginger (Gari or Shoga)

The ginger is used to cleanse the palate between bites of sushi. It does not take a lot of ginger to cleanse the palate, so that a small pile should be enough for several rolls. Pickled ginger can be bought in Asian food stores, but if you wish to make your own, try this recipe.

Ingredients

250g/8oz ginger root

90ml/3fl oz rice vinegar

2 tablespoons mirin

2 tablespoons sake

5 teaspoons sugar

1 Scrub the ginger under running water as you would a potato for baking. Blanch in boiling water for one minute and drain.

2 Combine mirin, sake, and sugar in a small pan. Bring to a boil, stirring until the sugar has dissolved. Cool.

3 Place the ginger into a sterilised jar and pour the cooled vinegar over the ginger. Cover and keep 3-4 days before using. Will keep refrigerated for up to one month.

4 The pale pink colour develops as it ages, however, you might want to add a small amount of red food colouring.

Nori, (seaweed)

After harvesting, the seaweed is dried, toasted and sold packaged in standard size sheets (19X21cm/7^1/$_2$X8^1/$_2$in). Once the sealed cellophane or plastic bag has been opened, nori should be eaten at once. If not it should be stored in a sealed container in a dry, cool, dark place to preserve its crispiness. Nori is particularly rich in vitamins A, B12 and D.

Nori belts are used on nigiri-sushi when the topping being used is likely to slip off the rice, such as omelette and tofu.

Simply cut of a strip of nori about 1cm/^{1}/$_2$in wide and wrap it around the topping and rice to secure it.

Tezu

Is a bowl of half sushi vinegar and half water, used to make it easier to handle sushi rice and toppings.

Sake

A colourless brewed alcoholic beverage made from rice that is legally defined as a rice beer. Its bouquet is somewhat earthy, with subtle undertones; it has a slightly sweet initial taste, followed by a dry aftertaste. Sake should be stored in a cool, dark place prior to opening, then in the refrigerator after opening. Very popular in Japan, it is the traditional drink served before eating sushi, and should be served warm.

Mirin

Mirin is know as sweet sake, and is generally only used for seasoning. If unavailable, sweet sherry makes a suitable substitute.

ingredients

Daikon radish

Is a Japanese white radish, available fresh in Asian foodshops, in sizes ranging from 15cm/6in to 90cm/3ft. It may be refrigerated for several weeks. Cut into very fine slivers, it is commonly eaten with sashimi and can be used as a substitute for nori seaweed. When it is minced, it can be added to soy sauce for different texture and flavour.

Tofu

Custard-like cake of soya-bean curd, about 8cm/3in square. Sold fresh in supermarkets, it will keep for several days if refrigerated and left in fresh water. Often used in nigiri-sushi as a substitute for sushi rice, or as a topping on the rice.

Sushi Rice

When it comes to sushi the rice is as important as the fish, and it takes years of training to learn how to make perfect sushi rice. There are different ways of doing it, but by following the directions on page 78 you will have a universally accepted and uncomplicated method of making the rice.

Sesame seeds

The white sesame seeds are roasted and used as an aromatic seasoning, while the black seeds are mostly used as a garnish.

Wasabi

Grown only in Japan, wasabi horseradish, when grated finely, is a pungent, refreshing pulp that removes unpleasant fishiness. Fresh wasabi is very expensive and difficult to obtain, so the best alternative is the powdered variety. Mix it with water to get a firm consistency. The wasabi purchased in tubes tends to be too strong and lacking that real wasabi flavour.

Mayonnaise

Not extensively used in sushi cooking, with the notable exception of the California Roll.

Instead of using the standard commercially-made egg mayonnaise, try this homemade variety with a slight Japanese influence.

3 egg yolks
1/2 teaspoon lemon juice
50g/1 1/2 oz white miso
1 cup/250ml/8fl oz vegetable oil
salt to taste
sprinkle of white pepper
a pinch of grated yuzu*, lime, or lemon peel

*Yuzu is a Japanese orange used only for its rind. Kaffir lime used in Thai or Malaysian food is an alternative, as is lemon or lime rind.

Instructions

In a bowl, beat the egg yolks and lemon juice with a wooden spoon. Continue to beat, adding the salad oil a few drops at a time until the mixture begins to emulsify. Keep on adding the rest of the oil, then stir in the miso and the seasonings.

Refrigerate before using.

Flat cuts

Sashimi cuts

There are 5 basic fish-cutting methods for sashimi and sushi, and a very sharp, heavy knife is indispensable to them all.

Flat cut (Hira giri):

This is the most popular shape, suitable for any filleted fish. Holding the fish firmly, cut straight down in slices about $^1/_2$-1cm/ $^1/_4$ -$^1/_2$inch and 5cm/2in wide, depending on the size of the fillet.

Thread shape (Ito zukeri):

Although this technique may be used with any small fish, it is especially suitable for squid. Cut the squid straight down into $^1/_2$cm/$^1/_4$in slices, then cut lengthways into $^1/_2$cm/$^1/_4$in-wide strips

Cubic cut (Kazu giri):

This style of cutting is more often used for tuna. Cut the tuna as for the Flat cut , then cut into 1cm/$^1/_2$in cubes.

Paper-thin slices (Usu zukuri):

Place any white fish fillet, such as bream or snapper on a flat surface and, holding quite firmly with one hand, slice it at an angle into almost transparent sheets.

Angled cut (sorigiri):

Ideal cut for sushi topping. Starting with a rectangular piece of fish, such as salmon or tuna, cut a trianglar piece from one corner, and continue slicing off pieces approximately $^1/_2$-1cm/$^1/_2$-$^1/_2$in thick.

angled cuts

How to eat sushi

A lot of Japanese do not know the correct way to eat sushi. Eating it as explained below will maximise the flavours and experience of this great food.

There are 2 ways to eat your sushi.

Method 1

1 Turn the sushi on its side and pick up both the side topping and the rice with chopsticks or fingers, thumb, index and middle finger.

2 Dip the end of the topping, not the rice, in soy sauce.

3 Put the sushi in your mouth with the topping side directly onto your tongue.

Method 2

1 Pick up some pickled ginger and dip it into the soy sauce.

2 Apply soy sauce over the topping, using the ginger as a brush.

3 Put the sushi in your mouth with the topping side directly on your tongue.

There is no set order in which the various kinds of sushi are eaten, but the nori-wrapped pieces should be eaten first, since the crispness of nori seaweed does not last long once, it comes in contact with the damp rice.

Don't soak it in too much soy sauce. The rice falls apart and the taste of soy will dominate. The same goes for wasabi and pickled ginger. Be very moderate, or else the taste of the topping and the rice will be concealed instead of complemented.

In modern sushi-shops you may be served any drink you like with your sushi, but saké and green tea are always obligatory. Saké is served warm, and before you eat - not while and not after. The tea on the other hand is served during the whole meal. Green tea is essential for the full enjoyment of sushi, it removes aftertastes and leaves the mouth fresh for the next serving.

Health and sushi

Sushi is praised by nutritionists as a balanced and healthy food, because it contains many nutrients, including some minerals and vitamins, which would be partially destroyed by cooking.

Rice

Rice is an excellent source of complex carbohydrates and dietary fibre. Dietary fibres play an important role in digestion, while the carbohydrates provide energy that is slowly released, therefore lasting longer. It is also a good source of niacin, protein, thiamin and iron.

Fish and seafood

All seafood is low in kilojoules, with fewer kilojoules than even the leanest chicken and meat. It is also an excellent source of top quality protein and minerals, including iodine, zinc, potassium and phosphorus. It is also rich in vitamins, especially the B group. The small amount of fat in fish is rich in Omega-3-fatty acids, making fish a great heart food. Omega-3-fatty acids from fish can stop blood clots forming and blocking off arteries, thus reducing the risk of heart attack.

Nori

Seaweed is an excellent source of iodine, calcium and iron which are all important in maintaining healthy blood and bone structure. It is also high in vitamin B12, which makes sushi a valuable source of this vitamin since it is normally only found in animal products.

Soybeans

The soya bean provides the best quality protein of all pulses. This is used to make tofu, soy sauce and miso. While containing some starch it also has a high amount of fat in the form of poly-unsaturated oil. It also provides dietary fibre, some B-group vitamins, and a range of minerals.

Wasabi

Provides an excellent source of vitamin C.

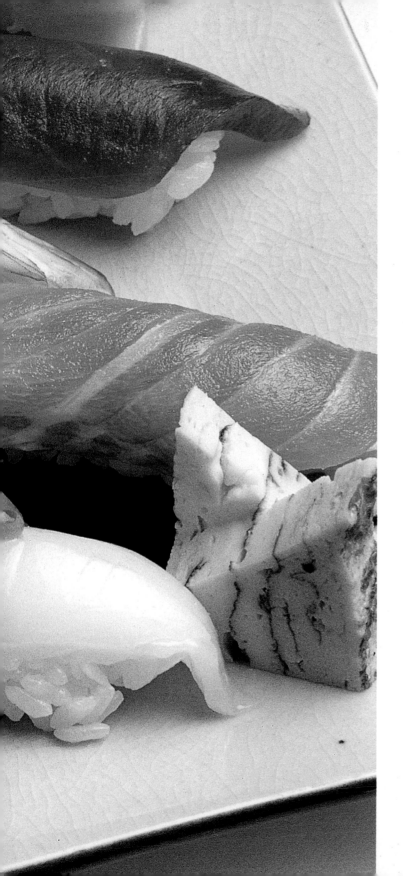

Nigiri-sushi ...

The word sushi alone commonly refers to "nigiri-sushi", a hand-shaped sushi commonly served at sushi restaurants. Nigiri-sushi is representative of Tokyo food and many varieties use some type of seafood or fish. The reasons for this might relate to the fact that the city (known as Edo prior to 1868) was rich in seafood of all kinds.

Nigiri-sushi with prawn (Ebi)

Instructions

1. Insert a bamboo skewer (15cm/5in long) through the prawn to prevent curling.

2. In a saucepan holding 2 cups of boiling water and the salt and vinegar, drop the prawns and simmer for 2-3 minutes.

3. Scoop out prawns and drop them into ice water. Refresh with cold water if necessary to ensure prawns are well chilled.

4. Twist skewer to remove prawns. Then shell prawns removing the legs and head, but leave the tip of the tail intact.

5. To remove the vein, slice lengthwise along the back and pull vein out.

6. Insert the knife along the leg side of the prawn and open like butterfly.

7. Soak in salted water for 20 minutes. Then transfer into a bowl of vinegar water and soak for further 20 minutes.

8. Proceed to make Nigiri-sushi as described on page 80

ingredients:

10 green king prawns
1 teaspoon salt
1 teaspoon vinegar
300g/100oz sushi rice
2 teaspoons wasabi paste
10 thin bamboo skewers
vinegar water
2 cups/500mL/16fl oz water
1 cup/250mL/8fl oz vinegar

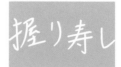

Nigiri-sushi with salmon (Sake)

Instructions

1 Pick up a piece of thinly sliced salmon fillet with your left hand between thumb and index finger. (see page 80/81)

2 Shape about 15g/¹/₂oz of sushi rice (bit smaller than golf ball)

3 Place a dab of wasabi in centre of the salmon with your index finger.

4 Put the rice onto the salmon.

5 Press the rice with your left thumb, it will leave a small depression in the ball.

6 Press the upper and bottom of the rice between the index finger and thumb of your right hand.

7 Press the surface of the rice with your right index finger.

8 Close the left hand gently then turn towards to right.

9 Now the topping should face upward. Then place index and middle finger on the topping.

10 Close your left hand then lift up gently.

11 Turn clockwise with your right index finger and thumb.

12 Press both sides then repeat steps 7-11 2 or 3 times

Note: One of the important criteria of well-made sushi is that the rice does not break when you pick it up.

Tips:

1 Most beginners hold too much rice . Hold less than you think you need.

2 Most beginners put too much water on their hands. Use only a small amount.

Makes 20 sushi

ingredients:
300g/10oz salmon fillet
300g/10oz sushi rice
1 tablespoon wasabi

Nigiri-sushi with tuna
(Maguru)

Instructions

Proceed as for Nigiri-sushi making techniques on page 80

Note: There several different varieties of tuna available both at the fish market, and also to the fisherman.

The 4 recommended types of tuna are:

1. Bluefin tuna is considered by most Japanese to be the superior fish in the tuna family.

2. Bigeye tuna is also highly regarded, only exceeded in price on the Japanese markets by the bluefin tuna.

3. Yellowfin tuna are extremely important and widely-resourced tropical tuna. It is air freighted, fresh chilled, to Japan but increasing quantities are now absorbed by Australian sashimi market.

4. Albacore is well regarded for sashimi, but quite high in calories. Often refered to as 'chicken of the sea' with its slight chicken flavour when cooked.

ingredients:

300g/10oz **tuna fillet**
300g/10oz **sushi rice**
1 tablespoon **wasabi**

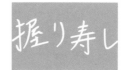
握り寿し

Opposite: Salmon sushi, prawn sushi

and tuna sushi

握り寿し

Cockle sushi (Maguru)

Instructions

1 Soak cockles in freshwater for minimum 3 hours to discard any sand.

2 Open cockles as you would for an oyster (page 98).

3 Proceed to make nigiri-sushi as described on page 80.

ingredients:
6 cockles in the shell
½ cup/75g/2½oz **sushi rice**
1 teaspoon wasabi

The cockle is a mollusc with two ridged oval shells hinged by a ligament near the pointed end.
Cockles are always sold in the shell, do not buy if open. They have a rich sea taste.

Opposite: cockle sushi (left) and seared scallop

sushi (right)

Nigiri-sushi with (Hotatagai) seared scallops

ingredients:
6 scallops
½ cup/75g/2½ oz **sushi rice**
1 teaspoon wasabi

Instructions

1 Sear scallops (either roe on or off, personal preference) on very hot grillplate or fry for 20 seconds each side.

2 Proceed to make nigiri-sushi as described on page 80.

Scallops are available in both half-shell and meat form. Shelling the scallop is simply a matter of sliding a knife between the scallop and shell and lifting apart.

marinated fish sushi (Zuke)

Instructions

ingredients:
300g/10oz **tuna (or bonito) fillet**
boiling water
½ cup/120mL/4fl oz **mirin**
½ cup/120mL/4fl oz **sake**
300g/10oz **sushi rice**
1 tablespoon **wasabi**

1   Place the tuna fillet on a cutting board over a sink.

2   Cover tuna with a cloth then pour the boiling water all over.

3   Put in cold water immediately.

4   Mix mirin and sake.

5   Wipe dry thoroughly, then put the tuna into the bowl with mixed sake and mirin.

6   Leave the tuna in marinade for about 2 or 3 hours.

7   Thinly slice for sushi or sashimi.

8   Make Nigiri-sushi as described on page 80.

Makes 20 pieces

grilled salmon belly sushi

ingredients:

200g/7oz **salmon belly skin on**

1 teaspoon **salt**

1 teaspoon **sake**

200g/7oz **sushi rice**

1 tablespoon **grated white radish**

2 teaspoons **soy sauce**

Instructions

1   Sprinkle salt and sake over the salmon's skin.

2   Grill on the skin side for about 2 minutes.

3   Remove from heat then leave until salmon cools.

4   Thinly slice and prepare as nigiri-sushi on page 80.

6   Place white radish on top of sushi as a garnish.

Note The salmon belly can be obtained from a fishmonger. Simply request it when he/she is next cutting up a salmon. The belly is a very tasty, if somewhat fatty, piece of the salmon.

Opposite: (L-R)Tuna zuke, sake toro, Bonito zuke

Nigiri-sushi with squid (Ika)

Instructions

1   Prepare squid as shown on page 98.

2   Cut the squid in the thread shape (Ito zukeri) as shown on page 13.

3   Proceed to make Nigiri-sushi as described on page 80.

ingredients:

300g/10oz squid

200g/7oz sushi rice

1 teaspoon wasabi

Nigiri-sushi with

seasonal white fish (Shiromi)

ingredients

**200g/7oz any white fleshed fish,
such as snapper, garfish or whiting**

200g/7oz sushi rice

1 teaspoon wasabi

Instructions

1   Cut the fish fillet paper-thin (Usu zukuri) as described on page 13.

2   Proceed as for Nigiri-sushi making techniques on page 80.

握り寿し

Opposite: (L-R) snapper sushi, whiting sushi

and squid sushi

Nigiri-sushi with sea eel (Anago)

1   Bring water to the boil, place eel in and allow to cook for about 1 minute and then refresh in cold water.
2   Add the sugar and soy sauce to the boiling water.
3   Place the eel back into the boiling water, cook for 20 minutes then remove from the heat.
4   Allow to cool and then proceed to make nigiri-sushi as described on page 80.
5   Wrap nigiri-sushi with nori belt

ingredients:
250g/8oz **sea water eel fillet**
450mL/15fl oz **water**
3 tablespoons **soy sauce**
3 tablespoons **sugar**
250g/8oz **sushi rice**
20 **nori belts**

Nigiri-sushi with freshwater eel (Unagi)

ingredients
½ cup/125mL/4fl oz **soy sauce**
1 cup/250mL/8fl oz **mirin**
2 tablespoons **sugar**
1 **pre-cooked unagi eel**
2 cups/300g/10oz **sushi rice**

Instructions

1   Combine soy sauce, sugar and mirin in a saucepan. Bring to the boil and reduce until half remains.
2   Thinly slice the eel and grill for 2 minutes, basting with the reduced soy sauce mixture.

Note: A fresh Unagi eel is very hard to obtain, and even harder to prepare. Asian supermarkets or a good fishmonger should have supplies of prepared Unagi eel.

Opposite: (L-R) Unagi sushi, and Anago sushi

Nigiri-sushi with
octopus (Tako)

Instructions

1   Cut head off and turn inside out.

2   Sprinkle 2 tablespoons salt over the octopus and rub
    into flesh. (This will remove the sliminess).

3   Have a large pot of boiling water at the ready, add
    2 tablespoons each of salt, sushi vinegar and the
    green tea. Boil the octopus for 8-10 minutes.

4   Remove octopus from boiling water and add to a pot
    of cold water that has been mixed with 2 tablespoons of
    salt and 4 tablespoons of sushi vinegar. Allow to sit for
    10 minutes.

5   Thinly slice the octopus and proceed to make Nigiri-sushi
    as described on page 80.

ingredients:

2 medium sized octopus
(approx 500g/1 lb each), cleaned
6 tablespoons salt
4 tablespoons sushi vinegar
2 tablespoons Japanese green tea (Ocha)
2 cups/300g/10oz sushi rice
15-20 nori belts

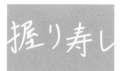

Opposite: (L-R) Octopus sushi, and cuttlefish

sushi

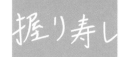

Nigiri-sushi with
leg of cuttlefish
(Geso)

ingredients:

1kg/2 lb **cuttlefish**

3 tablespoons **salt**

2 tablespoons **sushi vinegar**

1 tablespoons **Japanese green tea**
(Ocha)

1 ½ cups/210g/7oz **sushi rice**

10-15 **nori belts**

Instructions

1 Clean cuttlefish in the same manner as squid, as described on page 98.

2 Reserve the legs, using the hoods for tempura if desired.

3 Sprinkle 1 tablespoons salt over the cuttlefish and rub into flesh. (This will remove the sliminess).

4 Have a large pot of boiling water at the ready, add 1 tablespoon each of salt, sushi vinegar and the green tea. Boil the cuttlefish for 8-10 minutes.

5 Remove cuttlefish from boiling water and add to a pot of cold water that has been mixed with 1 tablespoon of salt and 1 tablespoon of sushi vinegar. Allow to sit for 10 minutes.

6 Thinly slice the cuttlefish and proceed to make Nigiri-sushi as described on page 80.

Nigiri-sushi with pickled
yellowtail (BohSushi)

Instructions

1   Fillet the fish as directed on page 97.

2   Sprinkle 2 tablespoons salt all over fillets, stand
    for 15-20 minutes.

3   Rinse in fresh water.

4   Place in bowl and cover with rice vinegar, stand for
    25 minutes then remove to a colander to drain.

5   Proceed to make Nigiri-sushi as described on page 80.

ingredients:

1 yellowtail (300-330g/10-11oz)

300mL/10fl oz rice vinegar

4 tablespoons salt

1 ½ cups/210g/7oz sushi rice

Chirashi Sushi

Instructions

The easiest type of sushi to make, made in all Japanese kitchens is "chirashi sushi", or scattered sushi. Chirashi-sushi is simply sushi rice with other ingredients mixed in or placed on the rice. Chirashi-sushi without any seafood often makes its appearance in lunch boxes. It's taken on picnics and often sold on railway station platforms. "Station lunches" are not exclusively chirashi-sushi but many are. Stations are known for their type of food as well as for their unique lunch containers in which they package their lunches. Again, the variations of this type of sushi are almost limitless. The rice can also be seasoned with a range of interesting ingredients such as chopped vegetables, sesame seeds, tofu pieces, chopped fresh and pickled ginger, crumbled nori and a variety of sauces.

suggestions for toppings
Tuna
Prawns
Omelette
Cuttlefish
Salmon
Unagi eel
Yellowtail
Bonito
Avocado
Tofu
Crab
Vegetables

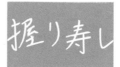

Tofu sushi

1   Cut the tofu

2   Mix the ginger and shallot , soy sauce

3   Add topping ingredients

4   Place the topping onto the tofu and tie with nori belt.

5   Put the mixed ginger on top then serve.

Note: The garnish already contains soy, so a bowl of soy and wasabi is not necessary

ingredients:
300g/10oz **tofu**
(substitute for sushi rice)
assortment of various fish
meat and vegetables
grated ginger
chopped shallot
1 teaspoon soy sauce
15-20 nori belts

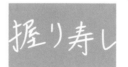

握り寿し

Opposite: Tofu sushi, with (L-R) Seared beef,

pickled yellowtail, smoked salmon

Maki-sushi ...

Maki-sushi is a "rolled sushi" with narrow strips of different ingredients (seafood, crisp vegetables or pickles) layered on a bed of vinegared rice and spread on a sheet of nori or seaweed, thus calling it "nori-maki sushi". Nori-maki is the most well-known and varied sushi because just about any ingredient can be rolled into the centre, from crisp vegetables and strips of omelette or strips of avocado.

Cucumber rolls (Kappamaki)

Instructions

Proceed to make cucumber rolls as described on page 82.

Note: You can further your variations from that which has been described here. Ingredients such as fresh salmon, smoked salmon, prawns, avocado, minced tuna with chilli, omelette and umeboshi plums can make exciting and tasty alternatives.

Makes 24 pieces

ingredients:

2 sheets nori (cut into half)
1 cup/155g/5oz sushi rice
4 pieces cucumber, each cut as strips
½ x 1 x 7½ cm (¼ x ½ x 3in)
1 teaspoon wasabi

thin sushi roll (Hosomaki)

Before making a sushi roll cut the nori into half, then cut the sheets so they have straight sides. The scraps can be used as nori belts.

Tuna rolls (Tekkamaki)

ingredients:

2 nori sheets
1 cup/155g/5oz sushi rice
4 pieces tuna, each cut as strips
½ x 1 x 7½ cm (¼ x ½ x 3in)
1 teaspoon wasabi

Instructions

Proceed to make Tuna rolls as described on page 82.

Makes 24 pieces

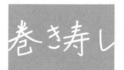

thick rolls (Futomaki)

ingredients:

4 nori sheets
1 tablespoon wasabi
3 cups/450g/15oz sushi rice
90g/3oz omelette
1 cucumber
1 ripe avocado
90g/3oz pre-cooked eel fillet

Instructions

1. Prepare the omelette, cucumber, avocado and eel by cutting into strips approximately $1/2 \times 1 \times 7 1/2$ cm ($1/4 \times 1/2 \times 3$ in) long.

2. Proceed to make thick rolls as described on page 84.

Makes 16 pieces

dynamite roll (spicy tuna)

ingredients:

4 nori sheets
1 tablespoon wasabi
3 cups/450g/15oz sushi rice
150g/3oz of tuna fillet, minced
1 teaspoon chilli bean sauce
(or Korean Kimchee to substitute)
30g/1oz shallots, chopped

Instructions

1. Combine tuna, chilli bean sauce and shallots.

2. Make rolls as described on page 84.

Makes 16

California roll

(Ura Makisushi)

Instructions

1   Shell and de-vein prawns, slice in half lengthways.

2   Make california rolls as described on page 84.

Makes 16 pieces

Variations: Clean one large carrot, cut in thick strips and blanch.
In salt water, blanch 90g/30oz english spinach, rinse in cold water,
drain and shake dry. Cut 90g/3oz fresh salmon fillet in finger thick
slices and marinate in Mirin. Prepare the California roll as
described.

ingredients:

4 nori sheets

3 cups/450g/15oz sushi rice

1 tablespoon wasabi

45g/1½ oz Japanese mayonnaise

4-8 coral lettuce leaves

4 medium cooked prawns or seafood sticks

1 ripe avocado, peeled, seeded and sliced

1 cucumber, cut into thin slices

8 teaspoons flying fish roe

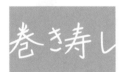

巻き寿し

inside-out roll (Sakamaki)

Instructions

1   Prepare the fillings for the rolls. Slice salmon, avocado and
     cucumber into suitable lengths.

2   Proceed to make your inside-out rolls as directed on
     page 86.

Note: Fillings can be varied depending on seasonal availability
of ingredients. Avocado is not always available, so choose
whatever suits your taste. Instead of flying fish roe on the
outside of the roll, sesame seeds, salmon roe or dried bonito
flakes make tasty alternatives.

ingredients:

4 nori sheets

3 cups/450g/15oz sushi rice

8 teaspoons flying fish roe

1 tablespoon wasabi

210g/7oz salmon fillet

1 ripe avocado

1 cucumber

Four-Sides Rolls
(Shikai maki)

Instructions

1   Place 1 sheet of nori on bamboo mat.

2   Spread one-third of the sushi rice.

3   Place another sheet of nori on top of first layer.

4   Spread another third of the sushi rice onto the nori.

5   Proceed to make sushi roll as described on page 84.

6   Cut the roll lengthways into quarters.

7   Place final sheet of nori on bamboo mat and spread last of the rice.

8   Turn the nori over and place onto a cloth, as described in 'Sakamaki' (page86). Place 4 quarters of the previously cut roll along side each other, place the omelette in the middle and proceed to roll.

9   Roll and form a square, press the grated egg onto the sides and then cut into four equal pieces.

Makes 4 pieces

ingredients:

3 nori sheets
250g/8oz sushi rice
Sushi omelette cut into a
1½ cm/½ in square
Kimi oboro
(Grated hard boiled egg yolk)

Temaki sushi

巻き寿し

Instructions

Temaki sushi originally was a meal for busy chefs. Having the ingredients on hand but no time to make sushi for themselves, they created this 'hand-roll sushi'. Temaki offers one more Sushi variation in a cone shape. Temaki offers a good way to experiment with ingredients such as cooked chicken, raw or rare beef, sometimes seasoned with flavoursome sauces. They are quick and easy to prepare and taste delicious, even with an inexpensive filling.

• If you cannot buy roasted nori sheets, you can roast them yourself. Lightly toast one side of the sheet of nori for about 30 seconds over a gas flame. Toasting both sides seems to diminish the taste. Or toast them in a frying pan without oil on low heat until the aroma comes out. The nori will be crisp and have a dark green colour after cooking.

• Leftover from roasted nori sheets can be chopped and used as a seasoning, or just to nibble on.

• If you make Temaki Sushi with soft or semi-liquid ingredients, it is easier with the rice at the bottom and the filling above it.

• In Japan the fresh sprouts of the Daikon radish are a popular ingredients for Temaki- and Maki Sushi. They resemble large mustard and cress, but are much hotter and spicier. They go well with Omelette Sushi. Daikon sprouts are available in Asian supermarkets and greengrocers.

ingredients:
10 nori sheets, halved
500g/1 lb sushi rice
wasabi

You can grow them as well at home from the seeds of the Daikon radish. Small Temaki Sushi is perfect as an appetiser, because they are easy to eat as finger food.

Suggestions for Fillings
Tuna slices
Spicy tuna (see page 42)
Tempura prawns (see page 112)
Teriyaki chicken
Cooked prawns
Crab sticks
Unagi eel fillets
Pickled whiting or yellowtail sashimi (see page 57)
Flying fish, salmon or sea urchin roe
Omelette
Cucumber
Avocado
Smoked salmon (or any smoked fish)
Instead of using wasabi, perhaps use Japanese mayonnaise or creamed cheese

Note: As an unusual variation or in case you ran out of nori sheets: Temaki Sushi may even be rolled in lettuce, particularly Cos (Romaine), or Iceberg. Lettuce makes a light, refreshing roll.

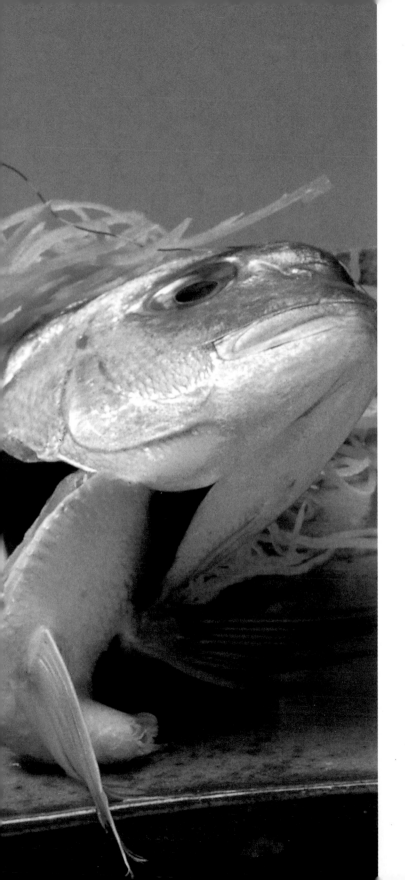

Sashimi...

The specialty of Japanese cuisine, fresh fish served raw. The fish, which must be utterly fresh, is sliced paper thin or alternately one-quarter to one-half inch (³/₄-1¹/₂ cm) thick, cubed, or cut in strips, according to the nature of the fish. The sashimi is accompanied by wasabi and soy sauce. Sashimi is always part of a formal Japanese meal, served early while the palate is still clear in order for its nuances to be appreciated.

Garfish Sashimi

(Sayori)

1   Clean, gut and fillet the garfish as described on
     page 97.

2   Cut the fillets into either the thread shape or
     paper-thin slices.

3   Arrange on plate and sprinkle with shredded nori.

Note: Garfish is a salt water finfish found all around Australia, but in more
concentrated numbers towards southern states. There are some 20 species
of this slender, silvery fish located in Australia. They are similar but can be
distinguished by the length of their 'beaks' and colour. It has a fine, sweet,
delicately flavoured flesh but care has to be taken to remove all of the bones.

ingredients:
2 whole medium sized garfish
shredded nori, for garnish

Pickled Whiting Sashimi
(Kisu)

Instructions

1. Clean, gut and fillet the whiting as described on page 97.
2. Sprinkle salt all over the fillets and allow to stand for 10-15 minutes
3. Rinse in fresh water
4. Place fillets in a bowl and cover with the rice vinegar, allow to stand for a further 10 minutes.
5. Remove from vinegar and drain in colander.
6. Cut the fillets into squares or paper-thin slices. (Page 13).

Note: There are some 6 different species of whiting in Australian waters. The King George and Sand Whitings are considered the more superior eating of the species. All whiting are very sweet and delicately flavoured. A 'peppery' flavour is sometimes apparent in the King George Whiting.

ingredients:
2 fresh whole whiting
2 tablespoons salt
1 cup/250mL/8fl oz rice vinegar

Trevally Sashimi (Shimaaji)

ingredients:
1 whole trevally, (approx 1kg/2lb)
shredded radish for garnish

Instructions

1   Clean, gut and fillet the trevally as described on page 97.

2   Cut the fillets into a 'flat cut', as directed on page 13.

3   Some paper-thin cuts may be cut and curled into a
    rose shape to make dish more attractive.

Note: There are several varieties of trevally available, but the smaller sizes
make the better eating as the large fish tend to be somewhat drier and
flavourless. Trevally has a firm, white flesh with a moderate 'fishy' flavour
and is an excellent , if somewhat underrated, fish for eating sashimi style.

Tuna Sashimi

(Maguru)

Instructions

1   Proceed to cut tuna into straight-cuts as described on page 13.
2   Put soy sauce, sake and dried bonito into a small saucepan and bring to the boil, stirring constantly, for 2 minutes.
3   Strain through a fine sieve and cool to room temperature. Divide dipping sauce among small dishes and serve with tuna sashimi.

Note: If the fillet you have purchased has already been cut into a 'block', you can proceed to cut the fish into the sashimi. If on the other hand, the fillet has not been trimmed and shaped into a block, then you may need to buy a larger fillet and trim it down to size yourself, perhaps using the off-cuts as minced tuna.

ingredients:
300g/10oz **sashimi-grade tuna fillet**
Tosa Juya (Dipping Sauce)
3 tablespoons **soy sauce**
2½ teaspoons **sake**
5 teaspoons **dried bonito (katsuobushi)**

Snapper Sashimi  (Tai)

1   Clean, gut and fillet the snapper as described on page 97.

2   Straight-cut the fillet or slice into paper-thin slices as described
    on page 13.

3   Arrange the shredded carrot and endive on the plate as a garnish.

Note: Snapper is generally recognised as one of our most highly regarded
foodfishes. Although very well known as cooking fish, the snapper is
coming into its own right as a sashimi style fish, being served in many
Japanese restaurants. It has a firm, white flesh with a sweet to mild flavour.

ingredients:
1 medium snapper (1¹/₂kg/3 lb)
shredded carrot
endive

Salmon Sashimi

(Sake)

Instructions

1   If purchasing a whole salmon, proceed to clean, gut and fillet the fish as described on page 97.

2   Trim away any dark or bruised flesh that may be evident, as well as any skin and 'fatty' flesh.

3   Shape the fillets into a block and apply the straight-cut, cutting off required number of pieces. (Any off-cuts of salmon may be minced, mixed with wasabi and used in Battleship Sushi).

4   Arrange on plate and garnish with shredded daikon radish.

Note: The Atlantic salmon is a highly valued fish for the table, both in cooked and sashimi form. Being a relative newcomer to the Australian marketplace, (thanks to the successful aquaculture industry in Tasmania) its rich, firm, succulent flesh has been well received.

Other varieties of salmon are available in Australia, but do not compete with the qualities of the Atlantic salmon.

ingredients:

300g/10oz **sashimi-grade salmon or**

1 whole salmon

shredded radish

Bonito Sashimi
(Katsuo)

ingredients:
1 whole bonito (2kg/4lb)
1 teaspoon ginger, grated

Instructions

1   Clean, gut and fillet the snapper as described on page 97.

2   Straight-cut the fillets (leave the skin on).

3   Arrange on serving plate, garnish with grated ginger.

Note: Bonito is a widely distributed fish, with varieties found around the world. The flesh is pink-red in colour with a beautiful coarse grain and a rich flavour. If purchasing in fillet form, look for firm, moist flesh and marbling. The nature of the colour is a good indicator of the freshness. A freshly cut surface is very dull.

Yellowtail Sashimi (Tatakin)

Instructions

1   Clean, gut and fillet the yellowtail as described on page 97.

2   Make sure all bones and skin are removed.

3   Fine-strip cut the fillets as directed on page 13.

4   Combine the yellowtail, ginger and shallots together and sit for about 30 minutes, allowing the flavours to set.

Note: Yellowtail is a member of the trevally family of fish, with a bigger reputation as a game fishing bait than that of a foodfish. Yellowtail is a very popular fish in Japan for sashimi, and its abundance and good value at the marketplace should see more yellowtail eaten here in Australia. The fillets tend to be somewhat dry and oily, with a medium flavour.

ingredients:
3 yellowtail
4 shallots, chopped
2 teaspoons ginger, grated

Scampi Sashimi

(Tenagaebi)

Instructions

1 To prepare scampi, remove heads and set aside for garnish.

2 Peel back the under-side shell from the top down to the tail.

3 Remove the flesh, discard the shells except bottom part of tail.

4 Place scampi meat on plate, putting head and tail on as garnish.

5 To make dipping sauce, warm sake in small saucepan then ignite it with a match, off the heat, and shake the pan gently until the flame dies out. Allow to cool.

6 Put sake with the other ingredients and mix well. Pour into individual bowls and serve with scampi or any other sashimi.

Note: The scampi, or deep sea lobster as it is also called, is targeted by trawlers mostly off northwestern Australia. They are generally snap-frozen on-board the trawlers; thus making the job of finding fresh specimens a lot more difficult. Scampi has a wonderfully sweet flesh, ideal for sashimi. It is considered by many to have eating qualities above that of the lobster.

ingredients:

8 scampi (if unavailable fresh, frozen is also good)

Chirizu (Spicy Dipping Sauce)

5 teaspoons sake

3 tablespoons freshly grated daikon radish

2 spring onions, finely sliced

3 tablespoons soy sauce

3 tablespoons lemon juice

1/8 teaspoon hichimi togarashi (seven-pepper spice)

Cuttlefish Sashimi
(Ika)

Instructions

1   Clean the cuttlefish in the same way as squid, which is described on page 98.

2   To make cuttlefish and cucumber rolls, cut cuttlefish and nori into a sheet 5x10cm/2x4in.

3   Score the cuttlefish at ½cm/¼in intervals.

4   Place scored cuttlefish face down, lay nori on top, then cucumber and flying fish roe.

5   Roll up and cut into 1cm/½in slices.

6   For cuttlefish and nori rolls, cut nori and cuttlefish into same size and place nori on top of cuttlefish.

7   Lightly score through the nori and into the cuttlefish and proceed to roll and cut into 1cm/½in slices.

8   Cuttlefish can also be cut up into the fine-strip cut, as described on page 13. Garnish with shredded nori.

Note: Cuttlefish is a mollusc and is generally smaller than a squid. They are highly prized in Japanese cuisine, with a flavour superior to that of the squid. When buying cuttlefish, look for firm flesh and undamaged bodies. Don't be put off by a broken ink sac, they are often broken when they are caught. Clean in the same manner as you would a squid.

ingredients:
6 cuttlefish (or squid)
3 nori sheets
1 cucumber, cut into slices 10cm/4in long
1 teaspoon flying fish roe

Lobster Sashimi

(Ise ebi)

Instructions

1   If lobster is purchased frozen, allow to defrost overnight in the refrigerator.

2   Remove the head and reserve for garnish.

3   Use poultry scissors to make a nice clean cut in the tail shell.

4   Pull the lobster meat out. Stuff the empty shell with shredded daikon radish for presentation. Cut the lobster into small sashimi slices.

5   Lay the meat on the daikon bedded tail, and serve.

Note: Traditionally, lobsters that were to be prepared as sashimi were purchased live and killed moments before being presented and served. The Japanese obsession with absolute freshness made this practise commonplace.

ingredients:

1 whole green (uncooked) lobster
endive
shredded carrot
shredded daikon radish

Techniques ...

All you need to know to assist you to become an accomplished home sushi chef.

Instructions

Rice cooked for sushi should be slightly harder in texture than for other dishes. You will need approximately one cup of cooked rice for each roll. It is easier and better to make too much rice than too little. Every recipe for sushi rice is different, but they all work. You might find a recipe on the bottle of rice vinegar, on the bag of rice, or on the package of nori.

Most recipes call for rinsing the raw rice until the water runs clear, but it can be avoided. The reason it is rinsed first is to remove talc from the rice. Most rice seems to be coated now with some sort of cereal starch, rather than talc, so rinsing could be omitted. They also suggest letting the rinsed rice drain in a colander, or zaru, for 30-60 minutes. It's up to you. The rice you use should be short-grained rice.

1   Wash rice until water is clear.

2   Combine the rice and water in a sauce pan and set aside to 30 minutes.

3   Bring rice and water to boil.

4   Reduce heat to very low and simmer for 10 minutes.

5   Turn it off heat and leave for 20 minutes to steam.

6   Make sushi vinegar (mix all ingredients in a pan over heat until dissolve).

7   Spread the rice on a baking tray and then sprinkle the sushi vinegar over the rice and mix it as if cutting. Use a fan to cool until it reaches body temperature.

4 cups/880g/32oz **short grain rice**
4 cups/1 litre/35fl oz **water**
< Sushi vinegar >
½ cup/125mL/4fl oz **rice vinegar**
4 tablesoop sugar
2 teaspoon salt
1 teaspoon soy sauce

preparing sushi rice (Shari or Sushi Meshi)

1

Rinse a Japanese wooden bowl (Hangiri)
or a flat wooden bowl with cold water
before you place in the hot rice.

2

Add the sushi vinegar to the rice,
pouring it over a paddle to help
evenly dispense the vinegar.

3

Mix the vinegar into the rice, being
careful not the flatten the rice.

4

Use a fan to help bring the rice back to
room temperature.

making nigiri-sushi

Instructions

Most important when making nigiri-sushi is the balance between the topping and the rice. It is handformed by gently squeezing the ingredients together. You need a chopping-board, a sharp knife, a bowl of vinegared water (tezu) in which to rinse the fingers, the fish and the prepared rice.

1

Prepare the tezu, which consists of half water, half sushi vinegar. Moisten fingers and palms with the tezu.

2

Pick up a piece of fish in one hand, and with the other a small hand-full of prepared sushi-rice. Gently squeeze the rice to form a block.

3

With the piece of fish laying in the palm of your hand, a small amount of wasabi can be spread along the fish.

4

With the piece of fish still in your palm, the rice can be placed on top of the fish. Use your thumb and press down slightly on the rice, making a small depression.

5

Using the forefinger from the other hand, press down on the rice, causing it to flatten.

6

Turn the sushi over (fish side up) and using the thumb and middle finger, squeeze the rice together.

7

Position fingers and hand as above, covering the fish and rice. Gently squeeze around the sushi. Repeat steps 5-7 twice more.

8

You should now have a piece of finished sushi, with the fish covering the firm rice.

thin sushi rolls (Hosomaki)

1

Cut one nori sheet in half lengthwise,
Use two pieces for making the sushi rolls.
Place nori shiny side down onto the mat.
Moisten your hands with some tezu.

2

Get a handful of rice from the rice-
cooling tub. Spread the rice over the
nori, taking care to do this evenly.

3

With your forefinger, spread the desired
amount of wasabi across the rice, starting
at one end and spreading it across the
middle to the other end.

4

Place tuna strips along the centre of the
rice, on top of the wasabi. Lift the edge
of the bamboo mat.

5

With fingers from both hands hold onto the mat and the filling. Wrap the mat and nori over the filling, making sure all ingredients are are evenly pressed.

6

Continue rolling, but applying a little more pressure to compact the rice. If needed, repeat the last step again to ensure the rice is pressed firmly and evenly along the roll.

7

Remove roll from the mat and place on a cutting board. Cut the roll in half.

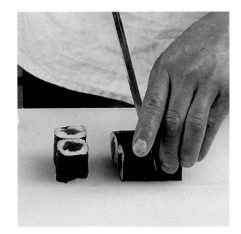

8

Generally allow 6 pieces per roll, so lay the 2 halves next to each other and cut into thirds.

巻き寿し

thick sushi rolls (Futomaki)

1

Lay I sheet of nori shiny side down onto the bamboo rolling mat, moisten your hands with some tezu and get a handful of sushi rice.

2

Spread the rice evenly over the surface of the nori.

3

Add the desired amount of wasabi along the middle of the rice.

4

And also some Japanese mayonnaise.

5

Add the fillings you wish to use, placing them in the middle and on top of the wasabi and mayonnaise.

6

Start rolling the mat up over the ingredients, stopping when you get to about 2½cm/1 in away from the end of the nori.

7

Lift the mat up and roll forward again to join the edges of the nori together, while at the same time applying a small amount of pressure to make the roll firm.

8

Using a sharp knife, cut the completed rolls in half, place the halves next to each other and cut into thirds. Each roll will provide 6 pieces.

inside out rolls (Sakamaki)

1

Have a nori sheet lying on a bamboo rolling mat and pick up a small handful of sushi rice.

2

Spread the rice out evenly over the nori. Once done, take nori and rice off the board and place on a damp cloth.

3

Place nori and rice onto the damp cloth and spread the desired amount of wasabi down the centre of the nori.

4

Add ingredients along centre of nori.

5

Start rolling the mat up over the ingredients, stopping when you get to about 2½cm/1in away from the end of the nori.

6

Lift the mat up and roll forward again to join the edges of the nori together, while at the same time applying a small amount of pressure to firm the roll.

7

Remove the completed roll from the mat and place onto a plate. Gradually spoon the roe around the roll until there is a sufficient coating of the roe on the rice.

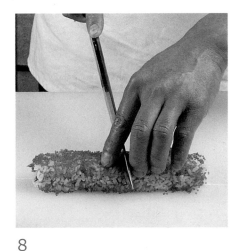

8

Using a sharp knife, cut the completed rolls in half, place the halves next to each other and cut into thirds. Each roll will provide 6 pieces.

temaki-sushi

1

Start by picking up a sheet of nori in one hand and a handful of rice about the size of a golf ball in the other.

2

Place rice on one side of the nori sheet and start spreading it out, remembering to cover only half of the nori sheet.

3

With your finger or a spoon, rub the
desired amount of wasabi along the rice.

4

Add desired fillings to the roll, placing
them from one corner down to the
middle of the opposite side.

5

Fold the nearest corner of the nori
over the filling, and start to shape into
a cone.

6

The finished temaki-sushi should be
coned shaped with no rice falling out
from the bottom.

battleship (Gunkan Makizushi)

1

Take a small handful of rice and mould it into a rectangular shape.

2

Wrap fingers from one hand around and over the rice. Position thumb from same hand at the end of the rice, while at the same time bringing the forefinger and middlefinger from other hand on top. Gently squeeze to make it firm and hold its own shape.

3

Cut a nori sheet into strips 1½in/4cm wide. This should give 5-6 pieces per sheet.

4

The hand holding the rice should be wet with tezu, and the other hand that is handling the nori should be dry. Position the piece of rice onto the nori strip.

5

Wrap the nori around the rice, and for holding the ends together, apply a little bit of tezu to make the roll secure.

6

Add the desired amount of wasabi with your finger.

7

Now the topping can be added. Spoon enough in until it reaches the top of the nori.

8

The Battleship sushi should be eaten fairly soon after making, since the liquid from the topping may drain through and some of the flavour will be lost.

sushi omelette

Instructions

1   Combine dashi, soy sauce, salt, sugar and mirin, stirring until sugar and
    salt have dissolved.

2   Beat in the eggs, being careful not to aerate the mixture if possible.

8 eggs
75mL/2¹⁄₂fl oz **dashi fish stock**
(available from Asian food stores)
3 tablespoons sugar
1 pinch salt
1 tablespoon mirin
2 tablespoons light soy sauce

1
Heat up the omelette pan (or ordinary
frying pan), adding a little vegetable oil
with a paper towel. Pour a little omelette
mix into the pan, allowing just a thin
layer to form.

2
Using chopsticks (or a spatular), try to
flatten out any bubbles that may appear.

sushi omelette

3

When it appears the omelette is almost cooked, or at least firm, tilt the pan up on its side, while at the same time slightly shaken the pan so the omelette becomes loose.

4

Using chopsticks, fold the omelette in half, bringing it from the elevated side closest to you down on top of the other half. Oil the pan again with a paper towel.

5

Add some more mixture to the pan.

6

Lift the cooked omelette and slightly tilt the pan, allowing the mixture to flow underneath. When firm, fold the omelette over as before.

7

Continue to add, cook and fold the omelette until mixture is used up

8

The end result. Note the layers of the omelette.

tempura batter

Japanese frying techniques are not unlike ours, but because of the close attention to the batter with which the food is often coated, and to the condition and temperature of the oil, Japanese fried foods are especially notable for their delicacy.

Note: The batter should be somewhat thin and watery, and easily run off a spoon. If it is too thick, thin it with drops of cold water. Ideally, the batter should be used shortly after being made, but may be used up to 10 minutes after being made.

1 egg yolk
1 cup/250mL/8fl oz **iced water**
4 ice cubes
1½ cups/185g/6oz **plain flour**

1

Add the egg yolk to a large bowl

2

Add water and ice cubes into the bowl with the egg.

3

Using chopsticks or a fork, beat the egg yolk and iced water until combined.

4

Sift the flour and add to egg and water mixture.

5

Mix well until ingredients are incorporated.

filleting

flatfish

Wash fish and leave wet as this makes it easier to scale. Remove scales using a knife or scaler and start at the tail and scrape towards the head.

Clip the dorsal fin with scissors or, if desired, remove both the dorsal and anal fins by cutting along the side of the fin with a sharp knife. Then pull the fin towards the head to remove it.

For boning or filleting, cut off the head behind gill opening. Use a sharp knife and cut-open belly from head to just above anal fin. Remove membranes, veins and viscera. Rinse thoroughly.

To preserve shape of roundfish, cut through the gills, open outer gill with the thumb. Put a finger into the gill and snag the inner gill. Gently pull to remove inner gill and viscera. Rinse well.

When skinning a whole roundfish, make a slit across the body, behind the gills, with another just above the tail. Then make another cut down the back.

Use a sharp knife, start at the tail and separate the skin from the flesh. Pull the knife towards the head, whilst holding the skin firmly with the other hand. Do not 'saw' the knife.

Place fillet skin, side down, and cut a small piece of flesh away from the skin close to the tail. Hold skin tight, and run a sharp knife along the skin

roundfish

To gut, make a small cut behind gills and pull out viscera.

Skin the whole flatfish, by first turning the dark side up and then cutting across the skin where the tail joins the body. With a sharp knife, peel the skin back towards the head until you have enough skin to hold with one hand.

Anchor the fish with one hand and pull the skin over the head. Turn fish over and hold the head whilst pulling the skin down to the tail.

Place skinned fish on chopping board with eyes up. Cut from head to tail through the flesh in the middle of the fish to the backbone. Insert a sharp knife between the ribs and the end of the fillet near the head. Pull knife down the fillet on one side of the backbone and remove.

Cut off the remaining fillet in the same manner. Turn fish over and remove the two bottom fillets.

preparing...

Oysters

If you use technique rather than strength, oysters are easy
to open. It is best to hold the unopened oyster in a garden
glove or tea towel (which will protect one hand from the
rough shell) whilst you open the shell with an oyster knife,
held in the other hand.

Hold the oyster with the deep cut down and insert the tip of
the oyster knife into the hinge, then twist to open the shell.
Do not open oyster by attempting to insert the oyster knife
into the front lip of the shell.

Squid and cuttlefish

Rinse in cold water and then cut off tentacles, just above
the eye. Squeeze the thick centre-part of the tentacles.
This will push out the hard beak, which you should discard.

Squeeze the entrails out by running your
fingers from the closed to the open end.
Pull out the quill and discard.

Peel-off skin by slipping finger under it.
Pull-off the edible fins from either side
and also skin them.

fish quality guideline

The most important thing when making sushi is that the fish is really fresh. Eel and octopus is always cooked.

Here are some guidelines on judging the quality and freshness of fish and shellfish:

- A fresh fish should have shiny and almost sparkling skin.
- Its body should be stiff and the meat firm when touched.
- Most fresh fish have clear eyes.
- The tail should not be dried out or curled up at the end.
- It should smell like the ocean (or like a clean pond if it's a sweetwater fish).
- It should not smell fishy.
- The scales on a fresh fish should adhere tightly.
- The gills should be cherry-red and should not have any white slime.
- Never buy what seems to be the last pieces of a fillet (try to get a piece of a new one instead).
- Most shellfish should have tightly closed shells.

- Sometimes mussels gape slightly, but they should close quickly when tapped.
- Oysters should always be closed and stored flat so that their liquids don't drain out.
- Try to make the fishmonger your last stop when shopping so you can rush home and put the fish in the refrigerator.
- At home remove whole fish from its wrapping and rinse it off with cold water before putting it in the fridge. If you're not going to use the fish within an hour arrange the fish on ice in colander over a large bowl. If you store the fish in a bowl with ice you might end up with the fish sitting in a puddle of water, damaging the fish.
- Shellfish, mussels and oysters should be kept in a bowl covered with a wet towel in the refrigerator.

the Sushi bar

Sushi isn't just for lucky people anymore. You can find it anywhere, including pre-packaged at the neighbourhood grocery.

But the best place to get the full flavour of the experience is still the sushi bar.

At first glance, the restaurant doesn't seem unusual. Some customers sit on floor mats at low tables, whilst others may choose a more traditional table.

However, if you want to be where the action is, sit at the Sushi bar. This is where the sushi chef holds court over a small mountain of seafood. All well displayed so you may inspect its freshness, colour and texture. Here you will find a myriad of whole fish and shellfish and sheets of kelp wrapping papers.

The chef – outfitted in a short-sleeved smock and a bright headband - is working non-stop magic with a ball of rice and the prettiest chunk of bright orange salmon you've ever seen.

Every so often a waitress walks by with a tray for the tables in the back. There are dark green, ice-cream-cone shaped Californian rolls, with fish and avocado in them, whilst other interesting rolls have fresh tuna or cucumber as their centre.

As you take a seat your chef or waitress will offer you a menu – usually with full colour photographs and descriptions in English. You'll also be offered something to drink, and you will face your first - and most important – test.

. . . . Try the sake.

Sake is a Japanese wine, made from fermented rice, and is traditional with fish dishes. It is potent, fragrant and faintly sweet. But before you begin, a word of warning: An empty cup is considered rude, so your host will keep the bottom wet. Turn the cup upside down when you've had enough.

Your place setting may cause you anxiety, but don't worry. As there are no knives and forks, you either learn chopsticks or resort to fingers. Both are acceptable. You'll find a small bottle of soy sauce (shoyu) and a shallow dish for mixing the sauce with a pinch of wasabi (Japanese mustard).

You will also find a small, mound of gari (ginger) in the corner of your platter. These paper-thin slices, pink and pickled, clear out the previous taste sensation and get you ready for the next one. Think of it as a reset button for your taste buds.

Chopsticks can be frustrating for first-timers. Just as you get the hang of clamping onto that rice block, you dip it and the whole piece disintegrates on the way to your mouth.

Try this: invert your sushi and dip the fish side in your shoyu mixture. After all, the idea is to complement the flavour of the fish, not the rice.

Now all you need to decide is what you'll order first. In this wide universe, there's a meal waiting for diners of all persuasions.

Quick tips...

for surviving a sushi bar

1 Sit at the sushi bar

It's the only way to get the full flavour of the sushi experience . . . and you can keep a close eye on the chef.

2 Looking for sushi sans fish

Vegetarians and others who aren't yet ready for seafood in the raw can turn on to kappa maki, omelet sushi and miso soup.

3 It's not all raw

Lots of sushi styles are cooked ... at least a little bit. But there are some fine distinctions. For instance: ebi (shrimp) is blanched. Ama ebi (sweet shrimp) is served raw.

4 Full disclosure

If full disclosure makes you more comfortable you might want to stick with the nigiri-sushi style: It's very straightforward - rice block, fish on top. You know exactly what you're getting into.

5 Caviar

Lovers of caviar will likely gravitate toward the gunkan-style "boat" sushi. This is where the truly exotic seafood lives from the insides of the spiny sea urchin to the eggs of the Japanese flying fish.

Sushi etiquette

Using Chopsticks

The chopsticks are picked up with the right hand and arranged for comfortable use with the left. Hold the chopsticks slightly towards the thick end. Reverse the tips of the chopsticks before you help yourself to a community dish. When chopsticks are not in use, return them to the right side of your dish.

At the Bar

First, the experienced sushi-eater will order assorted sashimi to give the sushi chef a chance to show off his best fish. Always ask the chief what's good. Sashimi is eaten with chopsticks as it is not fingerfood.

When done with the sashimi, ask for a change of soy dish. No wasabi should be placed in the dish, since wasabi is already between the rice and the fish. Now you're ready for nigiri-sushi. Nigiri is meant to be eaten with your hands, so don't waste time fumbling with your chopsticks. Lightly dip the end into soy sauce, then place the fish side onto your taste buds. Avoid biting the piece in half, just pop the whole thing in. He will look at your plate to see how well you are doing, rather than look at you for your next selection.

When finished, ask the waitress (not the chef) for the bill. Sushi men take pride in their job and a substantial gratuity should be left in their place.

Bad Manners

Do not ask for knives. This would imply that the food is so tough it can't be properly eaten without them.

Do not pass food to another person with chopsticks. This act parallels passing cremated bones of a deceased relative at a Japanese funeral.

Do not scrape rice from chopsticks.

Do not eat all the rice at once, rather, return to it after tasting other dishes. Rice when taken must always be eaten.

Do not wave your chopsticks around aimlessly over the food, trying to decide what to take next.

Wasabi

Don't use too much wasabi. Wasabi paralyses your palette and will hide the subtle flavours that fish has when eaten raw.

The sushi chef

Heir to the Samurai Tradition

The spirit of sushi is carried on over the centuries by "shokunin" (traditional master sushi chefs).

The Japanese are great believers in learning through apprenticeship. Before you are even allowed to pick up a knife you must work in the kitchen sweeping, doing dishes and other jobs for at least a couple of years. It may take ten years of training to be considered a master and become the head chef.

The sushi chef is heir to the samurai tradition and upholds the ideals of the samurai- they are scholastic and gentlemen of high personal standards and great self-discipline. They wear spotless ghi's and a knotted headband, evidence that they are serious about their work.

Sushi is considered an art and in a country where cooking is highly regarded as a profession, to be a sushi chef is considered an honour.

Tools

A sushi man's knives are as important to him as a sword is to a samurai. His knives are made from carbon-steel that can be sharpened to literally cut a hair.

A sushi man has his own set of knives which can cost several hundred dollars apiece. He sharpens them before and after use, cleans them after every few strokes, and wraps them up and keeps them in a safe place every night.

Contrary to most knives, sushi knives are sharpened on one side only which makes for a faster, cleaner cut.

Other types of sushi

Campbell roll

A Campbell roll contains salmon, asparagus, and mayonnaise. Use the smallest asparagus spears you can find, or cut larger ones into smaller strips like the cucumber. Cut the salmon into long strips about 1cm/$\frac{1}{2}$ wide by $\frac{1}{2}$cm/$\frac{1}{8}$-inch thick. The packages of smoked salmon you see in the deli sections of supermarkets are perfect for this. Spread some Japanese mayonnaise along the edge of the roll. Place the salmon on top of this, and the asparagus on top of the salmon, and use an amount approximately equal to the salmon.

Virginia roll

A Virginia roll contains crab, eel and mushrooms. Virginians prefer to use real crab meat, but imitation will work just fine.

Add the crab and eel, like the California, with the eel replacing the avocado. Mushrooms are then placed like the cucumber.

Saikuzushi

Saikuzushi, or festival sushi, is an art form. Rice is tinted different colours, sectioned off and rolled. When it is sliced, complex images are created.

Chakinzus

Chakinzushi is sushi rice in a thin omelette wrapper shaped and tied like a lady's drawstring purse. Sometimes a single pea or small shrimp decorates the ruffled part of the wrapper.

Fukusazushi

Fukusazushi is a variation of make-zushi, where the square-moulded rice mixture is wrapped in a thin sheet of omelette.

This is turned over to conceal the seams and garnished with a nori ribbon and ginger.

Temarizushi

Temarizushi are rice balls tightly wrapped in thinly-sliced marinated fish.

Preparing...

Stuffed Fried Bean Curd Bags (Inari-zushi).

Ingredients

1x10 packet thin deep-fried tofu (aburage)

$^2/_3$ cup/165mL/5$^1/_2$fl oz dashi broth

3 tablespoons soy sauce

2 tablespoons sugar

1 tablespoon sake

$^1/_4$ grated boiled carrot

1 tablespoon toasted sesame seeds

1 $^1/_2$ cups/240g/8oz sushi rice

Instructions

1   Cut aburage into halves and pull open the centre of the
    pieces, making bags. (like preparing pita bread).

2   In a saucepan, combine dashi broth, soy sauce, sugar
    and sake. Bring to the boil and simmer the bean curd bags
    for 10 to 15 minutes. Remove from heat, drain and cool.

3   Mix the sushi rice with sesame seeds and carrot.

4   Fill the bags with the rice mixture and roll the top of the
    bean curd over the rice to enclose it. Be careful not to
    add too much rice or the bags will split.

Makunouchi

Ingredients

1 cooked bamboo shoot
1 cooked mushroom
I cooked bean curd
2 prawns
1 grilled yellowtail or garfish
1 cooked king prawn
1 combination sashimi
1 nagashimono (Japanese sweet jelly)
1 makunouchi box
7 pieces makunouchi rice

The Makunouchi bentoo emerged in the Edo Period in Edo (now Tokyo) as the meal of choice during intermission at the kabuki theatre (the word "makunouchi" means the interval between acts). Makunouchi is now a standard type of obentoo available at train stations, with bentoo shops almost anywhere else. The sushi rice is shaped into little cylinders and sprinkled with sesame seeds.

Instructions

The ingredients are presented in a decorative lacquer box in combinations carefully arranged for artistic effect.

Makunouchi nigiri

(Nigiri-sushi styled Makunouchi rice)

Ingredients

1 ½ cups/240g/8oz sushi rice
I teaspoon roasted sesame seeds
1 sheet nori, for nori belts
steamed asparagus
sliced cucumber
assorted fish fillet
cuttlefish

Make 8-10 pieces Makunouchi rice with toasted
sesame seeds.

Place each of the ingredients in sushi-cut style on top of rice.

Wrap nori belt around the pieces that require it.

Note: Use any combination of ingredients that is available.

Sushi a la carte

aji — horse mackerel

akagai — ark shell

ama-ebi — raw shrimp

anago — conger eel

aoyagi — round clam

awabi — abalone

ayu— sweetfish

buri — adult yellowtail

chutoro — marbled tuna belly

ebi — boiled shrimp

hamachi — young yellowtail

hamaguri — clam

hamo — pike conger; sea eel

hatahata — sandfish

hikari-mono — various kinds of "shiny" fish, such as mackerel

himo — "fringe" around an ark shell

hirame — flounder

hokkigai — surf clam

hotategai — scallop

ika — squid

ikura — salmon roe

inada — very young yellowtail

kaibashira — eye of scallop or shellfish valve muscles

kaiware — daikon-radish sprouts

kajiki — swordfish

kani — crab

kanpachi — very young yellowtail

karei — flatfish

katsuo — bonito

kazunoko — herring roe

kohada — gizzard shad

kuruma-ebi — prawn

maguro — tuna

makajiki — blue marlin

masu — trout

meji (maguro) — young tuna

mekajiki — swordfish

mirugai — surf clam

negi-toro — tuna belly and chopped green onion

ni-ika — squid simmered in a soy-flavored stock

nori-tama — sweetened egg wrapped in dried seaweed

otoro — fatty portion of tuna belly

saba — mackerel

sake — salmon

sawara — Spanish mackerel

sayori — (springtime) halfbeak

seigo — young sea bass

shako — mantis shrimp

shima-aji — another variety of aji

shime-saba — mackerel (marinated)

shiromi — seasonal "white meat" fish

suzuki — sea bass

tai — sea bream

tairagai — razor-shell clam

tako — octopus

tamago — sweet egg custard wrapped in dried seaweed

torigai — cockle

toro — choice tuna belly

tsubugai — Japanese "tsubugai" shellfish

uni — sea urchin roe

Maki-sushi (sushi rolls)

ana-kyu-maki — conger eel-and-cucumber rolls

chutoro-maki — marbled-tuna roll

futo-maki — a fat roll filled with rice, sweetened cooked egg, pickled gourd, and bits of vegetables

kaiware-maki — daikon-sprout roll

kanpyo-maki — pickled-gourd rolls

kappa-maki — cucumber-filled maki-sushi

maguro-temaki — tuna temaki

maki-mono — vinegared rice and fish (or other ingredients) rolled in nori seaweed

natto-maki — sticky, strong tasting fermented-soybean rolls

negitoro-maki — scallion-and-tuna roll

nori-maki — same as kanpyo-maki; in Osaka, same as futo-maki

oshinko-maki — -pickled-daikon (radish) rolls

otoro-maki — fatty-tuna roll

tekka-maki — tuna-filled maki-sushi

tekkappa-maki — selection of both tuna and cucumber rolls

temaki — hand-rolled cones made from dried seaweed

umejiso-maki — Japanese ume plum and perilla-leaf roll

Other sushi terms

battera-zushi — oshi-zushi topped with mackerel

chakin-zushi — vinegared rice wrapped in a thin egg crepe

chirashi-zushi — assorted raw fish and vegetables over rice

Edomae-zushi — same as nigiri-zushi

gari — vinegared ginger

inari-zushi — vinegared rice and vegetables wrapped in a bag of fried tofu

neta — sushi topping

nigiri-sushi or nigiri-zushi — pieces of raw fish over vinegared rice balls

odori-ebi — live ("dancing") shrimp

oshinko — Japanese pickles

oshi-zushi — Osaka-style sushi: squares of pressed rice topped with vinegared/cooked fish

sashimi — raw fish (without rice)

shoyu — soy sauce

tataki — pounded, almost raw fish

tekka-don — pieces of raw tuna over rice

wasabi — Japanese horseradish

Favourites

If there is one word to describe Japanese cuisine, then it has to be "artistic", in its purest sense. No other cuisine is so in harmony with nature. No other accords food such awesome respect. No other prepares it with such an eye to detail. We have included some of the more well known examples of Japanese foods, try them perhaps as a follow up to some sushi and sashimi...

tempura

Prawn Tempura (photograph on page 110)

Ingredients

5 large green prawns
vegetable cooking oil
1 cup/120g/4oz plain flour
1 cup/240mL/8fl oz iced water
1 egg yolk

Instructions

1   Shell and de-vein prawns, then cut 4 incisions into the
    under-section of each prawn and straighten them out to
    open up the cuts.

2   Combine flour, egg yolk and iced water to make a batter
    (see page 94).

3   Dip each prawn in flour and then in batter (twirl it around
    to properly coat it), then drop into hot oil (200°C/400°F).
    Only fry 5 pieces of food at a time.

4   Fry until golden brown. Remove and drain, serve with
    tempura sauce and grated horseradish or lemon.

Note: Keep oil clean during cooking by using a perforated spoon
to remove food particles from oil as they appear.

Tempura Sauce

Combine soy sauce, dashi (fish stock) & mirin, in equal
quantities and boil for 20 minutes over low heat. Allow to cool.
Best if served chilled.

Serves 2

The recipe shown above by no means encompasses all of the
ingredients that may be used in a Tempura recipe.

Substitutions and additions might include:

$1/2$mm/$1/4$in thick slices of fish fillets, $1/2$mm/$1/4$in thick slices of
carrot, skewered sections of spring onion, small asparagus stalks,
$1/2$mm/$1/4$in thick slices sweet potato, and many other ingredients
from beans to snow peas (mange-tout) and egg plant (aubergine).

Japanese breakfast

(Chou-shoku)

Thetraditional breakfast consists of a bowl of hot boiled short grain rice mixed with raw egg, nori flakes and soy sauce.

This is a very simple meal, and should be arranged with side dishes such as Japanese pickles, bean curd and miso soup (miso-shuru). To the majority of Japanese, breakfast is not breakfast without this thick, aromatic soup.

Miso soup

250g/8oz **tofu**
100g/3oz **miso paste**
1/2 cup/120mL/4fl oz **dashi stock**
1 tablespoon **mirin**
1 **shallot, chopped**
4 cups/ 1 litre **water**

Instructions

1 Boil water with the dashi.

2 Mix the miso and mirin together and add to the boiling liquid.

3 Dice the tofu into cubes and place into the hot stock and heat on medium for 5 minutes.

4 Serve in small individual dishes sprinkled with chopped shallots.

Serves 4-5

Sukiyaki

(Japanese Hot Pot)

Ingredients

600g/20oz scotch fillet
100g/3oz Japanese cabbage
2 bamboo shoots (Takenoko)
4 shallots
1 carrot
100g/3oz Japanese mushrooms (Shii-take)
125g/4oz Tofu
60g/2oz piece of suet
100g/3oz rice noodles (vermicelli)
4 spinach leaves
2 baby corn or Japanese Hill vegetables
(bracken, carrots, daikon etc)
3 raw eggs

Sauce: Warishita

1 cup/240mL/8fl oz soy sauce
$\frac{1}{4}$ cup/60mL/2fl oz mirin
$\frac{1}{2}$ cup/120g/4oz sugar
pinch salt
1 cup/240mL/8fl oz chicken stock or dashi

Instructions

1   Slice the Japanese cabbage into 5cm/2in slices. Cut the shallots
    into approx. 7$\frac{1}{2}$cm/3in lengths and thinly slice the bamboo
    shoots and the fillet of beef. Cut the carrots into fine shreds
    and cut the tofu into small squares. Place mushrooms into
    warm water and soak for 10 minutes.
    Soak the vermicelli in a bowl of warm water for 30 minutes
    until tender. Roll the spinach leaves up and cut as shallots.
    Cut the baby corn cobs in half and set aside.

2   To make the sukiyaki sauce (warishita) combine the soy sauce,
    mirin, salt and stock in a saucepan and heat for 30 minutes
    on low heat.

3   Heat the frypan and place the suet in it. Use this to grease the
    base of the pan. Gently fry the beef pieces and the shallots.
    When tender, pour over some of the warishita sauce then
    add remaining ingredients (except the eggs) to the pan and
    continue to cook gently until tender.
    Repeat this cooking process until all ingredients are used.

4   During the frying process add some sake or water to the pan
    to prevent excessive flavour development of the warishita
    and to maintain a balance of flavours throughout the cooking.

5   To serve sukiyaki, place the beaten egg in a bowl and use
    for dipping the sukiyaki pieces into. The raw egg is optional
    and not always used by western people. Sukiyaki can be
    served from the pot into small bowls of rice.

yakitori

Ingredients

100g/3¹/₂oz chicken breasts, cut into 5cm/2in pieces
1 shallot, cut into 5cm/2in pieces
4 bamboo skewers

yakitori Sauce

3 tablespoons sake
¹/₂ cup/120mL/4fl oz soy sauce
¹/₂ cup/120g/4oz sugar
pinch of salt
dash konbu (kelp stock)

Instructions

1   Combine all Yakitori Sauce ingredients and cook 30 minutes
    on low heat.
2   Thread prepared chicken and shallots onto skewers.
    Grill over a high heat or coals, turning occasionally until
    the juices begin to flow.
3   Brush with Yakitori Sauce or dip into the sauce and continue
    grilling until cooked to your choice.

Note: In Japan a lot of chicken and meat parts are substituted as
desired eg; giblet, liver, heart etc.

Serves 1

Teriyaki

Ingredients

4 chicken thighs

3 teaspoons sugar

¼ cup/60mL/2fl oz **sake**

½ cup/60mL/2fl oz **mirin**

½ cup/120mL/4fl oz **light soy sauce**

Teriyaki Chicken

Teriyaki can be applied to a wide variety of meats and seafood. Teriyaki fish cutlets, prawns, beef and squid are just a few of these can be barbecued or grilled using this versatile marinade.

Instructions

1   To make marinade, combine sugar, mirin, sake and soy sauce.

2   Bone the chicken thighs, leaving skin intact.

3   Place chicken into a dish, add about half the teriyaki marinade and marinate for 6-8 hours.

4   Remove chicken from marinade and place on barbecue about 20cm/8in from moderate coals.

5   Cook for about 45minutes, or until cooked.

6   Add remaining marinade to a saucepan and reduce to about half.   Serve with the cooked chicken.

Glossary

Anago (sea eel)

Anago is marine eel, a leaner version of unagi, freshwater eel. It is always boiled first, then grilled. Because it is served with a special mixture made from sugar, soy sauce, and eel stock, no dipping sauce or wasabi is needed.

Buzuguri

Chunk-style octopus.

California Roll

Popular for beginning sushi eaters, California rolls are hand rolls of cooked crab meat, avocado, and cucumber.

Ebi (boiled shrimp)

Very popular on sushi menus for their sweet, fresh taste, ebi are prawns that are boiled in salted water, then shelled and spread into a butterfly shape leaving only the shell of the tails attached. They are usually eaten with wasabi and soy sauce.

Gari (sliced ginger)

A garnish used to freshen the palate between sushi plates, gari is ginger root that has been pickled in salt and sweet vinegar. For best results when buying gari for making sushi, select firm knobs with smooth skin.

Gunkan

Known as "battleship style" sushi, gunkan is a type of nigiri-sushi that is made by wrapping a band of seaweed around a pad of rice and pressed down so ingredients can lay on top. This is an easy way to serve fish roe and other smaller ingredients.

Hamachi (yellowtail)

Hamachi is a variety of yellowtail, which is a common name for amberjack. It is light yellow in colour and has a rich, smooth smoky taste. Sushi chefs consider the tail and the cheek of the fish the best part and this is often saved and cooked for special customers.

Hiro Special

Cream cheese, cucumber, crab, avocado, salmon, and tuna; this sushi is wrapped reverse style, with the rice on the outside.

Ikura (salmon roe)

These are the red shiny ball-like sushi. The name ikura derives from "ikra", a Russian word for fish roe or caviar. This is why ikura is sometimes used as red caviar in Australian cuisine as well as a delicious sushi dish.

Kani (crab)

Always served cooked, Kani is an excellent choice for sushi beginners. It can be enjoyed as nigiri-sushi or wrapped in seaweed as it is served in California rolls. Kani is real crab meat, while kanikama is artificial crabmeat, used sometimes for certain types of sushi.

Kyuri

Cucumber wrapped with seaweed.

Maguro (tuna)

Maguro is the most popular item sold at sushi bars due to its familiarity and fresh, clean taste. Though there are many varieties of tuna, yellowfin or bluefin lean cut tuna is what is used for sushi. If your've going to try to roll your own, chefs recommend experimenting with maguro sushi in the winter, when the tuna is at its peak.

Maki-sushi or maki sushi (rolled sushi)

A type of sushi made by wrapping rice, fish, and other ingredients into a long seaweed roll, then sliced into bite-sized pieces. There are two types of maki-sushi rolls: hosomaki, a slender roll made into 6 small pieces and temaki, a hand roll which is eaten in 2-3 bites and resembles the shape of an ice cream cone. Maki-sushi is served with soy sauce and gari.

Makisu

Used for preparing rolled sushi, a makisu is a mat made from bamboo sticks tied together with cotton string. If you're going to make rolled sushi, this is an essential tool.

Masago (smelt roe)

Masago are small orange flying fish eggs, and is a prized delicacy in Japan. Masago can be prepared as nigiri-sushi, gunkan, or maki-sushi and is often used for garnishing the outside of hand rolls. It is closely related to tobiko, a flying fish roe, and though slightly lighter in colour, it shares its taste: salty, and resistant to the bite.

Nigiri-sushi or nigiri-zushi

Meaning "pressed by the hand," nigiri-sushi is a slice of cooked or uncooked fish that lies across a pad of rice. The ingredients are then gently pressed together. Fish roe is also made into nigiri-sushi, in which case a strip of seaweed is wrapped around it to hold it together. Nigiri-sushi is often served with wasabi and is meant to be dipped in soy sauce.

Sake (salmon)

Salmon is a very popular kind of sushi, easily recognisable by its bright orange colour and sweet, tender flavour. Salmon is never served raw in sushi bars; rather, it is lightly smoked first or it is cured in salt and sugar for a few days and then served.

Glossary

Sashimi

Sashimi means "raw fish." It is eaten with no rice, though it is often dipped in soy sauce and eaten with wasabi and ginger. Sashimi is carefully selected from the purest waters and is prepared by specially trained sashimi chefs to ensure the highest quality fish. Sashimi is generally eaten at the beginning of the meal before the sushi.

Sonosan Roll

Cheese, cucumber, avocado, and tuna.

Sushi

Japanese staple that combines vinegar-flavoured rice with fish. Sushi comes in many forms and can be eaten with chopsticks or with your hands. The most common types of sushi are Nigiri-sushi (hand made sushi), and maki-sushi (rolled sushi made with a bamboo mat). Additionally, sashimi is raw fish that is very commonly eaten along with a sushi meal.

Suzuki (sea bass)

Japanese fish with shiny white flesh and mild flavour. Sometimes it is served as sashimi that is called "suzuki usu zukuri."

Tako (octopus)

Tako is recognisable by its burgundy tentacles; in fact, the legs of the octopus are actually more commonly eaten than the body. Tako is always boiled before served which tenderises the flesh and leaves the meat with a slightly chewy and subtly flavour.

Tekka Maki

A raw tuna and rice roll. The name "tekka" refers to the gambling parlours in Japan, where this snack was served at the gaming table as finger-food.

Unagi (freshwater eel)

Unagi is similar to anago (marine eel) in colour and taste. Instead of being boiled first, however, it is grilled, then glazed with a mixture of soy sauce, sugar, and eel broth. The sauce makes the flavour sweet and rich, and it should be eaten without any dipping sauce.

Uni (sea urchin)

For the brave sushi eater, uni is considered a delicacy in many parts of the world. What is actually served is the gonads of the sea urchin. Its soft texture, held in place with a band of nori, has a delicious, subtle, nut-like flavour and is a definite favourite among advanced sushi eaters.

Wasabi (horseradish)

A spicy green horseradish spread with a very pungent taste that helps to bring out the flavour of sushi.

Index

Index

Notes

Notes